Am I Weird?

Positive Mindset For Kids Series.

Story By
Cathy Domoney

Illustrations By
Moran Reudor

ISBN: 9781087287096

For Skye, Tristan, Noah, Caleb and Thea Rose:
Always be courageous in claiming your birth-right to be your quirky;
crazy; unique; inspirational and authentic selves.
Love Mama, xx

For Ian:
Thanks for being my super-fun, long-serving,
amazing partner-in-crime.
Love Doris. xx

Robyn was a beautiful girl with chestnut brown eyes
that sparkled like water, and feathers for hair.
She giggled and danced her way through life.
Robyn went to ballet lessons.
She loved to twirl and spin, leap and hop,
stretch and glide, she was in heaven.

Mr. Dazz told all of the girls to bring
their favourite doll to the next lesson.
Robyn squealed with delight,
she knew just who to bring...

The next lesson she took Ben, her favourite doll.
Ben was a brave soldier who liked to crawl through mud,
save his fellow toys and keep fit and strong.
Robyn was so excited to do her dance with Ben.
While she was waiting she noticed the other girls
in the class giggling and pointing at her.
The girls all had baby-dolls.
Robyn didn't mind at all, she thought
that everyone's dolls looked great.
She did her dance and beamed with delight.

"You're so weird," said the girls.

Christmas was fast approaching.
Robyn desperately wanted
the "Pirate Crushing-Bones" dress-up outfit.
He was so cool.

He had a massive black hat,
an eye-patch encrusted with jewels,
a big bushy beard (where birds would nest)
and a mighty sword to defend his shipmates.
He would always call
"Tis adventure we shall seek Me Hearties!"

Robyn the Pirate was at the shops when she noticed
a girl dressed in a stunning sparkling princess dress.
"Gosh, I really love your dress," Robyn said,
"You look so sparkly!"
The girl looked Robyn up and down aghast,
"You look ridiculous! You can't wear
a Pirate's outfit, you're a girl!"
"Of course I can! I'm wearing it now!"
laughed Robyn.
"You're so weird," the girl replied.
Robyn watched quietly as the girl walked away.

Robyn played soccer and was the only girl on the team.
On scoring the winning goal of the match,
her teammates lifted her up on their shoulders and cheered.
The losing team were not happy.
"You shouldn't even be playing soccer on that team!"
they told her. "You're so weird!"

At the beach with her family,
Robyn sat quietly watching the waves lick the sand.
"Dad, am I weird?" she asked.
"Why do you ask?" replied Dad.
Robyn shuffled in the sand,
"Because the other kids always call me weird
because of the things I like."
"Oh I see," said Dad,
"In that case, yes you are most definitely weird."
Robyn scrunched-up her nose
against the sunlight dancing on the water.
"What does weird mean exactly?" she asked.

"Weird means that you are strong and brave.
Weird means that you have the courage to be
who you are.
It means that you chase and embrace your happiness,
whether other people understand your choices or not.
Being weird gives other kids the hope that one day
they could be weird too.
We are so proud of you bug."

And dad hugged her tight in the salty sandy air.

A gigantic smile the shape of
a luminous crescent moon
broke out of Robyn's face
as her heart doubled in size.
She leapt up and ran in to
the water with all of her
clothes on dancing,
splashing and singing.

"You're so weird!" shouted Dad.
Robyn laughed wrestling with the water,
happy to be fully and wonderfully weird.

For Parents, Counsellors, Carers and Teachers:

I have included this section with some points to guide you in how to use this book as a tool with your children to discuss the important and sometimes difficult issues that arise in their lives.

Points To Share With Children:

- Ask your children how they think that Robyn felt in each situation where someone called her weird for following her own path.

- She did not seem overly concerned and she still had fun but sometimes she was quiet. What could she have been thinking in these situations?

- How would you have felt in this situation? Has this ever happened to you? What happened? How did it make you feel?

- What could you have done in this situation?

- Did you find it to be a positive experience? How could you have used this situation to make it positive for yourself? (For example: If someone laughed at you for what you were doing did you think that it was your fault and that you should change? Or, did you understand that this person is most likely too scared to do something different because they are scared to be different? Did you recognize how brave and free you are for being yourself?)

- Which public figures do you really admire? What is special and unique about this person? What makes them stand-out from the rest? Do you think that they would be where there are in life if they just decided to be what everyone else expected them to be? Food for thought!

- If you have ever felt uncomfortable about someone else's reaction to you, what do you do with those feelings? (It is so great to explore this and encourage the children to explore feelings words around this topic. For example: If you list the uncomfortable feeling-words there is an opportunity to revisit this situation and reframe it. 'I felt stupid' could be changed to' I was brave enough to do something different.' Etc.)

- A nice activity to do in order to get an insight into children's inner-wishes is to ask them to discuss/write/draw a response to the question: If you knew for sure that everyone would celebrate and support you in the decisions you made about your future life, what would you choose to do?

Suggested Activities.

- Locker/Drawer/Pillow Post: Write your children a secret letter to be placed under their pillow, or in their school drawer/locker. Tell them all the things that they are doing right. Let them know how proud you are of them and all the amazing things that you love and admire about them. I have done this with great effect. Sometimes a small, simple surprise such as this can have a significant and long-lasting positive impact.

- Dream Diary: Using words and pictures, write or draw in a special scrapbook all of the fantastic, wonderful things that your children think about themselves and all of things that they would like to achieve. This is a terrific focus for our children and a very positive way to help them to remain focused on goals (which can easily be adjusted over time, what you are establishing here is self-belief based on your belief in them. Our parent's voices often heavily influence the tone of our inner dialogue as we grow into adulthood.)

- Celebration Poster: A lovely activity for great self-esteem is to make a poster with your child's name at the center. Then family and friends can add all the wonderful skills, talents and attributes belonging to that child, all around their name. This promotes a feeling of uniqueness and of being special and important. I have used this within my own family as well as with classes full of children. It is a wonderful experience for all involved, the focus child often does not realize the good things that others feel about them. This raises their self-esteem and helps them to further live-up to the opinions of them help by others. Get creative! Use glitter, magazine pictures, color, stickers etc. The brighter the better! It is great to have as a back-up resource in the future if ever they have a down-day as it reminds them just how wonderful they are.

- Catch them being good at school: If you are working with a child who has very low self-esteem which has manifested itself in a deterioration of their behavior, it is very important to focus on every single thing that they get right. For example, one boy who I inherited in my new class when I used to teach had reached the point of being excluded from school. One bad choice followed another relentlessly. He had been labelled as a troublemaker, and he lived up to his hype! We started his self-esteem journey by creating a sticker-chart for every playtime he had for the whole week, every week. Every playtime, he was awarded a sticker for having chosen to play nicely with someone new (as he had no friends). He was also rewarded for having made it through the playtime without having physically hurt anyone in any way. We decided upon how many stickers would be his realistic target to achieve. If he met his weekly target, a celebration poster was sent home to his very supportive single parent at the end of the week. It was astounding how quickly this child made progress. Why? Because as the adults in his life, we cared, we wanted him to succeed, we believed he could do it, and we made sure that he could achieve and celebrate it. Every kindness, every polite word, every good choice, no matter how small, was celebrated. He lived up to the expectations and the praise, and his behavior and his academic progress began to improve. Parents could share this approach with teachers and suggest that they try it.

- Catch them being good at home: These collected stickers could become a voucher to cash in for money, a trip to the park, chocolate, a cinema trip—whatever your budget and your agreement with the child. An important note about the giving of stickers is that once given, they should never be taken away as a punishment. If a bad choice is made, think of another consequence like an early bedtime, no TV, etc. Never take away what the child has worked so hard to earn, otherwise this undermines the whole process, and the child is likely to give up. Also, whatever the voucher represents must be realistic, as it must be delivered to the child upon completion as the reward.

- Flip It!: Sit with your child and scribe for them all of the things that they are worried or unhappy about, and turn them into statements. Then one by one, flip those statements from negative to positive. For example, "People do not like me" becomes "I am strong inside. I am a clever, funny person who makes good choices, and people want to be my friend." Often these changes in our thought process affect the way that we act around others, the way we think about ourselves; our general behavior changes for the better. Therefore, our expectations and the expectations o those around us change for the positive. These affirmations, when used regularly, are simple and yet can be very effective. The affirmations will evolve as the child grows and their aspirations change. These can be read aloud and shared every morning and night.

- Separate the child from any 'bad' behavior: If your child has been having difficulty with their choices and behavior, it is important for them to face the consequences and accept responsibility for what they have done. (Please note that some adults have difficulty in achieving this!) However, it is very important that it is their behavior that is labelled and not their character. If your behavior is labeled as 'bullying' for example, behavior can be easily changed through guidance on how to make good choices. If the child is labeled as a 'bully-character' then this is a harder position to shake and change from. It gives people the impression that that is who they are, rather than a reflection of some bad decisions that they made. Once this has been done, they must be allowed to move on and leave it behind. This means that the decision or incident is not to be refereed to again by anyone if possible. The new and improved behaviors and choices are to be referred to and encouraged as much as possible to reinforce and anchor them. If there is a 'slip' in their behavior, then they can be reminded through the Celebration Poster/Pillow or Tray Mail etc. who they really are and help them to find their way back to that state of being.

- As the adult, your role is to be clear about what to expect from the child, as well as the rewards and sanctions that have been agreed upon and put in place. The child needs to feel safe while they put the changes in place, so they need to be clear and consistent about what they are needing to do. They need a supportive environment in which to learn about positive and negative consequences. Implementing safe and fair sanctions is an expression of love. You are helping the child to understand about reasonable behaviors, accountability and consequences. These are lessons they will need to successfully function in the outside world.

- Always ask what their side-of-the-story is and listen, listen and listen some more. It is so vital to have empathy of where they are coming from (even if they are wrong!) They need to feel that they have been heard, understood and that their feelings have been considered. I have found that when they feel valued in this way then the end-result is always so much more positive and successful (even if the result is the implementation of sanctions!)

- Please remember that none of us are perfect -not even me!! (Don't tell anyone!!) Some days will be better than others; there is no such thing as a perfect teacher/parent/carer etc. Be kind to yourself, do everything with an open ear, an understanding soul and a loving heart and remember that we are all looking for acceptance and connection.

- Celebrate your young person for who they are today; get excited about who they will become tomorrow and provide a safe environment for them within which they can make mistakes and grow and watch them blossom!

Lovely Friends,

Thank you so very much for buying my book, I am so delighted that you are here! I have the best readers who often contact me via email and social media to give me the amazing feedback on how my books have positively impacted the lives of the children in their care. Please do feel free to reach out and contact me with a photo of you and your cherubs holding my book, I would love to see you! Am I Weird? is based on the experiences that I had with my first-born daughter Skye and how we fully encouraged her quirkiness and how it was received by those around us. Skye has always been fiercely herself (as have all five of our children) and this has been celebrated by us but has not always been easy to navigate as a parent when over the years some others have resisted Skye's individuality. For me, the courage to be yourself is sacred, incredibly precious and should be encouraged and protected at all costs!

I do hope that you and your children have enjoyed this particular book in my 'Positive Mindset For Kids' series and that you are able to use it as a platform for starting important conversations with your young fledglings.

Other titles in the series include:

Pop Finds His Smile.

The Magic Is Inside You

Flip! Flop!

I Am Perfectly Me!

Dear Bully...

Coming Soon... Five Sonny Summers.

Thank you again for joining me on this journey and for encouraging your child to be their unique and perfect selves.

Warmest Regards,
Cathy. X

About The Author.

Cathy Domoney of Miracle-Ready Mindset is a professional Mentor (www.miraclereadymindset.com) and Inspirational Speaker, focusing on the power of mindset and its miraculous impact on the lives of her international clients. Originally with a background in teaching, Cathy became passionate about self-esteem and confidence work with adults and children alike. She holds Diplomas in Hypnotherapy and Counselling, and also holds a Bachelor's Degree in Sociology and Life Coaching. Cathy discovered early on in her teaching career how vital a person's view of themselves and their capabilities were to their academic attainment, behavior and happiness and how positive thinking powerfully impacts a child's experience in the world. Cathy's mission is to raise the confidence of as many children as she can through her stories and help them to achieve the individual greatness that each child has inside of them. She hopes that this can contribute to a much happier, more well-rounded future generation. Cathy's books are game-changers as she tackles the more complex social subjects and breaks them down into accessible and easy to understand stories. Cathy's mission is to expand minds, connect hearts and start important conversations. A best-seller on Amazon in the Education section, Cathy's 'Positive Mindset For Kids' Series has been very successful and well received and is being used by parents; carers; counsellors; teachers; psychologists and professionals who work with young people as a tool to open a dialogue about the important issues with their children.

To contact me for interviews or to connect please see below:

www.miraclereadymindset.com

miraclereadymindset@mail.com

Facebook: @cathydomoneybliss

Facebook: @cathydomoneyconfidentkids

Twitter @domchick

LinkedIn/Instagram Cathy Domoney